D0839750

HOGARTH'S
CHILDREN

First published 2007
© Hogarth Arts, The Foundling Museum

ISBN 978-0-9554063-1-7

HOGARTH'S CHILDREN

Edited by
Robin Simon

Exhibition curated by
Katherine Field

Published to accompany the exhibition at the
Foundling Museum, London
29 March-1 July 2007

HOGARTH ARTS
2007

CONTENTS

COVER: *Moses brought before Pharoah's daughter*, 1746 (detail)
Oil on canvas, 272.7 x 208.3 cm
The Foundling Museum, London

What's in a name?
The naming of the Foundling Hospital children

KATHERINE FIELD

1 *Christ and the Apostles* by William Hogarth (1697-1764). 1744
Ink and bluish wash on paper. 17.8 x 20.3 cm
© Royal London Hospital Archives. Courtesy of Royal London Hospital Archives

It was the night of 25 March (Lady Day) 1741. After years of struggle, Thomas Coram's vision of a Foundling Hospital for London's abandoned children was a reality. The permanent premises would not be completed for another few years but now the first children were being accepted under the watchful eye of a select company of governors, which included William Hogarth. Women filed in, passing under the shield that Hogarth had painted to be hung over door, to have their children inspected before admission. This prcoedure was intended to check that every child was less than two months of age and free of any infectious diseases. Records for each child were meticulously kept, noting physical details, what they were wearing, and any notes or tokens that they had pinned to their person. Child no. 32 was described as, 'A female child of about 5 weeks old, a fine Holland cap neatly tyed with a black ribbon, a pair of fine white Holland sleeves, a pair of cotton white stockings, and white brocaded silk shoes tyed with a white ribbon and a paper'.[1] An accompanying note is still pinned to her record sheet, which survives in the Hospital's archive, reading, 'I am the daughter of Samuel Wilde water gilder who died ye twentie fourth of February last I was born ye twentie forth of march. Pray let my Christian name be Alice.'[2]

The baptism of the children who had first been taken into the Hospital took place on 29 March 1741, when it is recorded:

> There was at the ceremony a fine appearance of persons of quality and distinction: his Grace the Duke of Bedford, our President, their Graces the Duke and Duchess of Richmond, the Countess of Pembroke, and several others, honouring the children with their names, and being their sponsor's.[3]

The book recording the number of each child, its new name, and the giver of that name, survives today, and is surprising in the unusual choices it reveals. Historically resonant names such as those of William Shakespeare, Inigo Jones, Owen Tudor, Thomas Cranmer, and Oliver Cromwell appear, as well as that of Francis Drake, which was chosen by Thomas Coram, who was himself a retired sea captain.[4] This latter choice also reflects the fact that many of the male children would one day make their living at sea.

Other favourite names were chosen from heroes and heroines of contemporary fiction, notably, on one occasion, 'Pamela Andrews' from Samuel Richardson's epistolary novel *Pamela, or Virtue Rewarded*, published in 1740. This latter child was lucky enough to survive childhood (many did not) and is later recorded as being sent as an apprentice to Ellen Harbet of the parish of Tadley, Hampshire, in 1761.[5] Another of Richardson's heroines, Clarissa Harlowe, of the eponymous novel, published in 1748, also makes an appearance. Both female characters were idealized examples of virtuous behaviour, which no doubt suggested them as excellent choices for Foundling children.[6] There is also a 'Tom Jones', himself a foundling, and the hero of Henry Fielding's novel of the same name published in 1749.

Names might also provide clues about the individuals responsible for bestowing them. Among the more interesting examples it that of the child named 'Houghton Hall',which was the choice of Sir Robert Walpole, Earl of Orford, England's first 'Prime Minister'. Walpole is listed as a Governor in the initial Foundling Hospital Charter of 1739, and Houghton Hall was his stately home in Norfolk, a superb mansion built in the fashionable Palladian manner. Some of the names are much more obvious, such as 'Thomas Coram' and (after his wife) Eunice Coram, who both named children after themselves. Because of the high mortality rate, however, there were several children successively called Thomas Coram, as two of them died quite early on. William Hogarth and his wife, Jane, each named a child after themselves: Hogarth named child no. 195 on 24 February 1744, while Jane named child no. 265 on 5 October 1746.

Intriguingly, Hogarth named a Foundling child after Daniel Lock (1684/5-1754) on 5 October 1746. Lock is quite an obscure character, thought to have been an architect, but to whom no existing buildings can be attributed. He was evidently a man of substantial means, however and his portrait by Hogarth (Pl 2) also appeared as a mezzotint (Pl 3). Lock was appointed a Foundling Governor on 29 December 1749 and Hogarth's portrait of himwas probably painted

2 *Daniel Lock* by William Hogarth, ?1752
Oil on canvas, 91.5 x 71.8 cm
Herbert F. Johnson Museum, Cornell University
Bequest of David Goodstein, Class of 1954

3 *Daniel Lock* by James McCardell
after William Hogarth
Mezzotint
David Alexander

in 1752. The question of why Hogarth chose Lock's name in particular may be due to another another event that took place in the year 1746, which was the foundation of the Lock Hospital, established specifically to treat the poor suffering from venereal disease.[7] This new hospital was in Lanesborough House, Hyde Park Corner, and began to admit patients on 31 January 1747. As an avid supporter of so many medical institutions, it seems likely that Hogarth found Lock an especially appropriate individual to be honoured in this way.

The register of names remains a fascinating insight into the social history of the period, reflecting as it does personalities who were at the forefront of the national consciousness, or who were considered to have played important roles in the history of the hospital itself. As a last and most fitting example there is the case of a young boy who was given the name 'Frederick Prince' on 7 April 1751.[8] There can be no doubt that this was in memory of the immensely popular Frederick, Prince of Wales, himself a supporter of the Foundling Hospital, who had died just over two weeks before.[9] This was indeed an illustrious name for a young Foundling to live up to, and reflects the optimism of the Foundling Hospital supporters in their hope that these children might grow up to be worthy citizens of the nation.

1 London Metropolitan Archives A/FH/A/9/1/1.
2 Ibid.
3 LMA *Daily Committee Minutes*, p. 7.
4 Child no. 483, baptized 2 April 1749.
5 From 25 March 1741-31 December 1752, of the 1040 children accepted, 471 had died. This was considered a remarkably low percentage considering the nearly 100% mortality rates of the Parish poorhouses.
6 Pamela's employer, 'Mr. B', eventually marries her in order to possess her, very much against the custom of the day, when it was expected that you would marry within your social class, unless of course it was for money. See, for example, Hearth's *Marriage à la Mode*. Clarissa was more unfortunate, defending her virtue only to be raped by Lovelace, the young gentleman who had tricked her into escaping with him from an arranged marriage. She subsequently dies. Many of the Foundling Hospital children were the offspring of mothers who had 'lost their virtue' and also been abandoned by the child's father. These unfortunate women would often be disinherited by their families, or, if in service, would lose their jobs. As a result, they could not afford to keep their children.
7 Ronald Paulson. *Hogarth: His Life, Art, and Times*, 1971, p. 58.
8 Brian Taylor, 'A portrait of Daniel Locke by William Hogarth', *The Antiquaries Journal*, 77 (1997), pp. 401-6.
9 His name appears as a Governor in the Charter (dated 17 October 1739).

II

Hogarth and the children of the poor

MARTIN POSTLE

Hogarth, more than any other artist, demonstrated through his art and his actions a profound sympathy for the child. Nor is it entirely a coincidence that the period in which Hogarth flourished witnessed a sea change in society's attitude towards children, and, indeed, the very concept of childhood. This change was related closely to the more prominent role of the child in family life, and the cultivation of childhood 'innocence'. By the early decades of the 18th century children were encouraged, at least in enlightened circles, to be seen – and also to be heard.[1] Among the moneyed and educated classes, a 'permissive' outlook towards family life evolved, where childhood was celebrated as special and distinct phase of life, with its own rituals and rites of passage. As a result adults became enmeshed increasingly in the art of child rearing, in children's education, in their sports activities and in their play. As the eminent historian JH Plumb noted, the children of the well to do were considered increasingly as 'luxury objects upon which their mothers and fathers were willing to spend larger and larger sums of money, not only for their education, but also for their entertainment and amusement'.[2] The effect upon the image of the child in an age of conspicuous material consumption is easy enough to find in the sphere of Georgian portraiture. And here, Hogarth's pioneering role is beyond question.

1 *The Cholmondeley family* by William Hogarth (1697-1764), 1732. Oil on canvas, 71 x 90.8 cm. The Marquess of Cholmondeley

2 *The Grey children*, 1740
Oil on canvas, 105.5 x 89.5 cm. St Louis Art Museum

Early in his career, in 1730, Hogarth produced a pair of pictures of children at play (National Museums & Galleries of Wales, Cardiff), known today as 'The House of Cards' and 'The Tea Party'. In the pictures the children mimic the polite rituals of adults, although, as the second picture makes clear – via the upturned table and shattered crockery – in the world of the child, things seldom turn out as planned. Indeed, in many of Hogarth's children's portraits disaster is only a step away, whether it is the impromptu appearance of the tabby cat on the back of a chair in *The Graham Children* (National Gallery, London) which threatens anarchy in an otherwise orderly ensemble, or the imminent collapse of a pile of books, in *The Cholmondeley Family* (Pl 1) due to the destructive antics of an energetic boy. Hogarth was also willing to make more pointed allusions to the more disturbing characteristics of children. In a picture of 1740, for example, *The Grey Children* (Pl 2), the three-year old son of the Earl of Stamford smiles sweetly while holding a writhing puppy by its hind legs, his inattention to the animal's discomfort suggesting the casual cruelty of which children are capable. Such devices, of course, belong in part to well-established allegorical traditions, where the trivial actions of children foreshadow the more serious events that befall adults, or indeed, the transience of life itself. But Hogarth wanted to do more than follow tradition, and, as Elizabeth Einberg has stressed, 'his truly innovative contribution was to combine – sometimes daringly – the visual language of time-honoured symbolism with representations of uncompromisingly "modern" real life'.[3] In terms of his visualisation of children it was not, perhaps, the children who inhabit the sphere of polite portraiture that provide Hogarth's keenest insights into real life, but the children of the poor.

Through the portrait it is possible to trace the evolution of attitudes towards children from polite society. Portraits provide valuable information on dress codes, etiquette and family values. Yet, when we consider the children of the poor, the picture is far less clear. Poor children rarely feature in the visual arts prior to the 18th century, and when they do – as in Marcellus Laroon's *Cryes of the City of London Drawn after the Life* of 1687 – they appear as mere appendages, part of the baggage dragged along by wretched parents (Pl 4), useful only as a means of soliciting charity, or as a ready source of cheap and exploitable labour. As the example of Thomas Coram and others demonstrate, by the mid-18th century a more caring attitude towards the poor was in evidence. Even so the abject poor – those reduced to the state of habitual begging to secure their existence – continued to evoke fear and suspicion, notably via the persistence of the the legend of the Beggar's curse. As the poet William Shenstone observed: 'If anyone's curse can effect damnation it is not that of the Pope but that of the poor.'[4] The children of the poor did not in the general public's perception exist as individuals but as part of an amorphous mob. And when the mob appeared on the streets of the capital, children, as well as women, played a prominent role.[5] As one contemporary observed, poor children were tantamount to a plague, 'lousing like swarms of locusts in every corner of the streets'.[6] Similarly, the poet, William Cowper, was disturbed by the nocturnal spectacle of 'children of seven years old [who] infest the street every evening with curses and songs'.[7]

During the first half of the 18th century a genre new to British art emerged which, in effect, provided polite society with the means by which to visualise the poor in a way that made them more palatable: this was the 'fancy picture'. The fancy picture embraced all sorts of people who lived on the margins – from street urchins to peddlers, prostitutes, maid

3 *Invitation to the game of pelota* by Bartolome Esteban Murillo (1617-82), *c*.1670. Oil on canvas, 164.9 x 110.5 cm. Dulwich College Picture Gallery

4 *The London Begger* by Marcellus Laroon (1679-1772). Engraving Private collection

servants, and old beggar men. The most popular subjects, however, were children. As a genre the fancy picture found it roots in the earthy character studies of Caravaggio and his followers, which injected a new sense of realism into both sacred and secular subjects. In the present context, however, perhaps the most significant figure, is the 17th-century Spanish artist, Murillo, whose paintings of beggar children (Pl 3) gained increasingly popularity among 18th-century British collectors, as well as notable artists such as Gainsborough and Reynolds. Among Hogarth's own contemporaries, however, it was the French painter, Philip Mercier, who made the fancy picture very much his own, with countless character studies of serving maids, ballad-sellers, courtesans, and winsome female street vendors.

Among Mercier's most popular fancy pictures was *The Oyster Girl*, which like many of his images was reproduced in engraved form for mass consumption. In this image Mercier drew upon a well-established European tradition that linked the trade of the oyster girl with her own potential as a desirable commodity – oysters being renowned for their aphrodisiacal qualities. Despite the fact that Hogarth must have been keenly aware of the popularity of the fancy picture, not least in the form of the reproductive print, it was not a genre that he explored in his own art. A possible exception may be the oil sketch, known today as *The Shrimp Girl* (Pl 7). The girl – clearly a teenager – has a notable pictorial precedent in Laroon's images of eel and crab sellers from the *Cryes of the City of London* series, although as Judy Egerton affirms, Hogarth's inspiration for the picture must have come directly from a girl whom he had seen in everyday life.[8] As has also been remarked, she relates also to several characters found in Hogarth's satirical works, notably the milkmaid in *The Enraged Musician* and the fishwife in *Beer Street*.[9] However, despite the possibility that *The Shrimp Girl* was intended as a study for one or other of Hogarth's narrative subjects, the very size of the

5 *The Four Times of the Day,* 'Morning', by William Hogarth, 1738. Engraving. Private collection

6 *A Rake's Progress,* 4, by William Hogarth, 1735. Engraving (second state). Private collection

image, and its concentration upon the girl's vibrant expression, suggests that Hogarth considered the image as a subject in its own right, as a form of 'fancy picture'. The picture, which remained unfinished, was never engraved during Hogarth's lifetime. However, in 1782 the Italian printmaker, Francesco Bartolozzi, made a stipple engraving of the painting. Tellingly, he altered Hogarth's original image by softening the girl's features and endowing her body with an air of sensuality through the insertion of an exposed nipple on her breast, entitling his print 'Shrimps!' – which may not have been intended merely to allude to her familiar street cry. Bartolozzi's subversion of Hogarth's image may seem trivial, but it underlines that fact that the fancy picture could at times be used to gratify fantasies about the pliability of the poor, and thus become a debased genre. At best, the fancy picture provided a sanitized view of the poor, presenting them as 'colourful' characters in alluring circumstances – figures of fun rather than as a collective threatening presence. Viewed in this context, it becomes easier to understand why the fancy picture held little attraction for Hogarth. In his art and in his life Hogarth had an abiding mission to highlight the true condition of the poor, not least poor children, whom he wished to represent not as an isolated species but as integrated – for better or worse – into the very fabric of society. Indeed, Hogarth's own troubled childhood, and the deprivations he had endured during his youth, prevented him from conceiving children as figures of fantasy or 'fancy', but as real flesh and blood presences – however uncomfortable that may have been for his contemporaries.

The most striking aspect of Hogarth's treatment of children in his narrative paintings is the way in which they are integrated into their environment, a world, moreover, in which adults and children mix freely, indicating that they are part of the same social sphere. Throughout, Hogarth is at pains to reveal that the way in which children live (and die) is as a result of the

7 *The shrimp girl* by William Hogarth, *c.*1745. Oil on canvas, 63.5 x 52.5 cm. National Gallery, London

behaviour of the adults around them, whose harsh experience of the world, all too quickly extinguishes their childish innocence. Hogarth accepts that children are often treated as marginal figures in the world of adults, yet does not treat them as mere bystanders. An early instance is the presence of the young boot-black in scene 4 of *A Rake's Progress*, where the eponymous rake is arrested for debt. In the original painting and in the first state of the print, a young boy stands at the extreme left of the composition, all but invisible to the other protagonists in the scene. Dressed in a long ragged tunic he carries his stool and basket over his arm. As the startled rake steps out of sedan chair, the boy deftly catches the rake's gold-tipped cane as it falls from his grasp. In the second state of the print (Pl 6) Hogarth replaced the single child with a group of seven boys, boot-blacks, liquor vendors, and newspaper hawkers, who smoke and gamble on the kerbside – at once providing a more vivid insight into seamy street culture of the London urchin.[10] At other times, poor children in Hogarth's narratives are portrayed as abject victims or 'captives' – in the sense that they have no opportunity of attain physical or mental freedom. Nor is the viewer spared any sense of their physical or mental suffering. Among the most poignant characterisations of this kind is that of the servant boy in 'Morning' in *The Four Times of the Day* (Pl 5). The scene is set in Covent Garden Piazza, outside Tom King's Coffee House, which forms a 'profane' contrast to the sacred environs of St Paul's church. Here, on an icy winter morning a couple of rakes indulge in a groping session with two wenches, observed in fascinated silence by a pious old maid, who shields her interest with a suitable look of contempt. Her air of moral superiority is undercut further by the presence of the snivelling servant boy who carries her prayer book. What is remarkable, aside from the sheer mastery of characterisation, is the immersion of the boy in an environment riddled with debauchery and violence. Nor can he derive any comfort from his employer, whose pinched features suggest a coldness of heart to rival the heat generated by the adjacent scenes of unbridled passion.

Throughout his characterisations of children, Hogarth suggests that the transience of childhood is further threatened by the intervention of adults, all too ready to exploit and despoil any vestige of innocence. Significantly, Hogarth adopts this stance at the very time that polite society prided itself upon its enlightened attitude toward the child – or at least the fortunate children who were the offspring of polite society. In doing so, he dares to expose far more than mere ignorance or insensitivity. Indeed, among those vices that Hogarth alludes to in his narratives involving children, the most harrowing is that of sexual abuse. Today, the subject of child abuse does not have comic connotations. In the 18th century, however, it was still regarded by some, alongside cock-fighting and bear-baiting, as a form of sport. And street children, as well as animals, were seen alike as fair game. A lewd ballad, *The Ladies Whim-Wham*, for example, celebrates the adventures of 'two frolicksome gentlemen' with a young boot-black, who 'with his catcher they both went to play / The Boy who was master indeed of the game / He tossed it, and catched it without any pain'.[11] The true extent of the pain and suffering which such encounters visited upon both the children involved, and upon society in general, was revealed by Hogarth in a scene from his most celebrated 'modern moral subject', *Marriage A-la-Mode*. Indeed, it is a scene so disturbing that its full ramifications are still insufficiently understood today.

Scene 3 of *Marriage A-la-Mode* is entitled 'The Inspection' (Pl 8). Judy Egerton notes, in her catalogue entry on this picture for the National Gallery, that the precise meaning of the scene has continually eluded commentators, who have failed to agree on an explanation of the nature of the matter at hand, or indeed the relationship between the four protagonists; the doctor, the older woman by his side, the Earl (having succeeded to his father's title), and his child-mistress.[12] It is clear, even from a rudimentary reading of the narrative, that the scene concerns the failure of the doctor to provide a satisfactory cure for the Earl's venereal disease. Less obvious, but resolved by Egerton, is the identity and role of the older woman. Infected, like everyone else in the scene, with venereal disease, she is a convicted prostitute (as a now near-invisible tattoo above her left breast indicates). She is also the mother of the child at the Earl's side, the connection between the two being revealed by Hogarth through the presence of the exact same material on the woman's sleeve and girl's skirt (indicating that she has used it to make garments for both of them).[13] The woman, therefore, is not only a procuress but one who is willing to make a prostitute of her own child. While this fact is disturbing, the most chilling feature of the picture is the age of the girl, a pathetic creature of no more than twelve years of age. As Henry Fielding had observed, many prostitutes were 'under the age of eighteen, many not more than twelve, and these, though young, half eaten up with the foul Distemper'.[14] Yet, I would suggest, Hogarth's reason for including a child-prostitute was not merely to heighten the sense of horror inherent in this scene, but to highlight one of the reasons why men, who may not have otherwise turned to children for sex, did so when infected by venereal disease.

André Rouquet, one of the most reliable commentators upon Hogarth's 'modern moral subjects' (since his information was based upon conversations with the artist) stated that the meaning of the 'Inspection' related to a quarrel between the Earl and the procuress over the poor health of the child 'du commerce de laquelle il n'est pas bien trouvé'.[15] In other words, it is the girl, and not merely the pills, that has failed to provide satisfaction. As another contemporary commentator noted, the procuress had guaranteed 'in her novices immature

8 *Marriage A-la-mode*, 3, 'The Inspection', by William Hogarth, *c.*1743-5.
Oil on canvas, 69.9 x 90.8 cm. National Gallery, London

youthfulness, innocence, complete ignorance of Gallicism of any kind, and therefore complete security'.[16] Yet, as the Earl points out, the girl, like him is infected with venereal disease, and is using the same pills. Even so, given that the Earl already has the disease why should he worry about contracting it from the girl? The answer, surely is that the girl was proffered not as a means of avoiding contamination but as a cure for his disease.

As the historian Antony Simpson, has observed, one major cause of the sexual abuse of young girls in the 18th century was the popular belief that sexual congress with them provided a cure for VD. As Hogarth would have been deeply aware, not least through his involvement with the Foundling Hospital, child rape was a major issue in London, which was the 'venereal, as well as the administrative, capital of the country'.[17] Between 1740 and 1744 – at the very time that Hogarth produced *Marriage A-la-Mode* – 50% of the prosecutions for rape involved victims under the age of ten (that is two years below the then legal age of consent), while in the 18th century as a whole some 25% of rape victims were children.[18] In 1746 the Lock Hospital was established in London for the specific treatment of venereal disease. In its initial report the Lock stated that over the preceding six years more than 50 children had been treated in London for VD. Significantly, the reason given was 'a received opinion among the lower people, both male and female, that if they have commerce with a sound person, they will not get the disease'.[19] Nor was this urban myth restricted to the poor or the ignorant, a London newspaper reporting as late as 1777, during the trial of a clergyman for paedophilia, that quack doctors continued to claim that 'if such a horrid act is committed on a child, that the person indisposed will entirely be freed from the disorder'.[20]

In 'The Inspection', Hogarth tackled the distasteful subject of venereal disease. The real focus of this bitter satire is, however, the more harrowing issue of child abuse: a far cry from the world of the artist's polite child portraits. The latter images featured the offspring of friends or favoured patrons. As such, these children formed an unusually privileged coterie, emblems of an age of enhanced sensibility, in which the 'new child' was a focus of unprecedented interest and affection. In his seminal text of 1693, published some four years before Hogarth's birth, John Locke had considered the mind of the child in a new light: as a *tabula rasa* 'white paper, or wax, to be moulded and fashioned as one pleases.[21] In his scheme for an 'enlightened' mode of education, superstition was banished and reason encouraged – alongside sports and games, an interest in music, science and the visual arts. And yet, as Hogarth reminds us, in the hard-hitting imagery of his 'modern moral subjects', the Lockean scheme impacted upon only the smallest sector of society. And while the outlook for the middle and upper-class child might have improved during this period, for the vast majority of children – as Hogarth knew only too well – life remained a cruel lottery, in which routine brutality, infanticide, disease, hard labour, and the predatory sexual behaviour of adults were endemic.[22]

1 See Phillipe Ariès, *Centuries of Childhood*, London 1962, passim.

2 J.H. Plumb, 'The New World of Children in Eighteenth-Century England', *Past and Present*, May 1975, p. 90.

3 Elizabeth Einberg in *Pictures of Innocence. Portraits of Children from Hogarth to Lawrence*, exh cat., The Holburne Museum of Art, Bath, 2005, p. 29.

4 Keith Thomas, *Religion and the Decline of Magic. Studies in Popular Beliefs in Sixteenth- and Seventeenth-Century England*, London, 1971, p. 605.

5 See Robert Shoemaker, *The London Mob. Violence, and Disorder in Eighteenth-Century England*, London, 2004, p. 138.

6 Hugh Cunningham, *The Children of the Poor: Representations of Childhood since the Seventeenth Century*, Oxford, 1991, p. 22.

7 Cunningham, op. cit., p. 23.

8 See Judy Egerton, *National Gallery Catalogues. The British School*, London, 1998, p. 182.

9 See Frederick Antal, *Hogarth and his place in European Art*, 1962, p. 117.

10 For the alterations to the various states of this print see Ronald Paulson, *Hogarth's Graphic Works. First complete edition*, 2 vols., New Haven and London 1965, vol. 1, pp. 165-66, vol. 2, pls. 143-44 and 246-47.

11 Quoted in Sheila O'Connell, *London 1753*, exhibition catalogue, British Museum, London 2003, p. 147.

12 See Egerton, op. cit., p. 163.

13 Egerton, op. cit., p. 164.

14 Loc. cit.

15 See Martin Postle, 'Hogarth's *Marriage A-la-Mode*, scene III. A re-inspection of 'The Inspection', *Apollo*, November 1997, pp. 38-9.

16 Lichtenberg's *Commentaries on Hogarth's Engravings*, translated from the German and with an introduction by Innes and Gustav Herdan, London, 1966, p. 104.

17 Antony E. Simpson, 'Vulnerability and the age of female consent: legal innovation and its effect on prosecutions for rape in eighteenth-century London', in G.S. Rousseau and Roy Porter, eds., *Sexual underworlds of the Enlightenment*, Manchester, 1987, p. 192.

18 Simpson, op. cit., p. 191.

19 Edward J. Bristow, *Vice and Vigilance; Purity Movements in Britain since 1700*, Dublin, 1977; Simpson, op. cit., p. 193.

20 *The Morning Chronicle*, 1 August 1777, quoted in Simpson, loc. cit.

21 See Roy Porter, *Enlightenment. Britain and the Creation of the Modern World*, London, 2000, p. 340.

22 See Linda Pollock, *Forgotten Children: Parent-Child Relations from 1500 to 1900*, Cambridge, 1983, pp. 262-71.

III

Children by Hogarth and Rysbrack

ROBIN SIMON

1 *Charity children engaged in navigation and husbandry*
by John Michael Rysbrack (1694-1770), 1745
White marble relief, Court Room, Foundling Museum

William Hogarth (1697-1764) was closely involved with the Foundling Hospital from its inception. The Hospital received its Royal Charter in October 1739, when Hogarth had already completed painting the head of Captain Coram, which was published as a mezzotint by James McArdell on 17 October (Pl 6). The full-length portrait itself (Pl 7) was presented in April 1740, by which date Hogarth was himself a governor of the Hospital. He was a very active governor. Although childless, Hogarth and his wife Jane (they called each other, and were known to intimates as, 'Billy' and 'Jenny') took in foundlings as foster children (until the age of five). Billy and Jenny also acted as inspectors of the wet-nurses who were employed to feed the infants.

Hogarth's practical attentiveness towards the children cared for by the Foundling was matched by his equally practical, objective, but unusually sympathetic, approach to the representation of children in this prints and paintings. Attitudes towards children had been profoundly affected by the thinking of the philosopher John Locke in the latter part of the pre-

2 *Edward Salter aged six* by John Michael Rysbrack (1694-1770), 1748
Terracotta, painted, ht 41.5 cm. Ashmolean Museum, Oxford
Photo courtesy Daniel Katz

vious century, especially in such writings as the famous *Essay Concerning Human Understanding* (1671) and *Some Thoughts Concerning Education* (1693).[1] The Foundling Hospital itself can be seen as an embodiment of the influence of Locke, while Hogarth's depictions of children are an unusually early instance of the influence of Locke's thinking upon the visual arts, something only paralleled in the period by Hogarth's associate, the sculptor Michael Rysbrack (1693-1770).

Rybsbrack donated the magnificent relief carving for the Court Room chimney-breast (Pl 1), *Charity children engaged in navigation and husbandry*, the subject of which shows those trades into which they would usually be placed. Rysbrack was the first artist, after Hogarth and George Frederick Zincke, to become a governor of the Hospital, which he did late in 1745, to be followed on 31 December 1746, when the Foundling Hospital finally moved into its handsome new building, by a group of other artists. All were expected to donate some example of their

3 *George Osborne, later John Ranby, Jr,* c.1748-50
Oil on canvas, 63 x 56.5 cm
Tate Britain

work for the adornment of the institution, and their gifts ranged from decorative plasterwork and carving in wood and marble to sculptures, landscapes and history paintings. Hogarth's colleague, the sculptor Louis-François Roubiliac, is conspicuous by his absence during this formative period, and in certain key respects Hogarth drew at least as much inspiration from Rysbrack as he did from Roubiliac to whom he was personally so close. One area in which this debt is especially evident is the portrait bust in a roundel or oval, a format in which Rysbrack was pre-eminent. Another, of particular interest in the present context, was small portrait busts of children.[2]

Hogarth's delightful portrait of John Ranby in the present exhibition (Pl 3) is a striking instance of the relationship that existed between Hogarth and Rysbrack in the 1740s. There seems little doubt that the portrait of John's sister Hannah (Pl 4) was originally conceived and executed in a much more traditional format (which is visible beneath the present decorations), and that it was only later overpainted by Hogarth to conform with the innovative pres-

4 *Hannah Ranby, Jr, c.*1747/50
Oil on canvas, 63 x 56.5 cm
Tate Britain

5 *John Barnerd,* by Michael Rysbrack, 1743
Terracotta, ht 37.5cm. Signed and dated
Private Collection. Photo: Christie's Images

entation of her younger brother, who appears within a fictive marble decorative surround. This 'carved' framework positively comparison with a sculpted bust. Hogarth is determined to offer a dramatically different image from anything that a sculptor, as opposed to a painter, might have supplied: he shows the boy in especially bright colours, and the whole illusionistic image is created with a marked – and visible – freedom of the brush. Yet, at the same time, Hogarth contrives to make the implicit comparison with sculpture unavoidable. His 'carved' frame cuts off the boy's arms below the shoulders, which ensures that the shape (as well as the general air) of this bust exactly imitates that of, to take a key example, Rysbrack's terracotta bust of the six-year-old Edward Salter created in 1748 (Pl 2), in all probability (taking into account the boy's age and that of his sister) two years before *John Ranby* was painted. Rysbrack had been cornering the market in charming busts of small children in the 1740s, and Hogarth was always inspired to keep up with, when he was not actually leading, the latest developments in art. Another example of which Hogarth would, in the normal run of events, have also been aware, is Rysbrack's terracotta of *John Barnerd*, modelled in 1743 (Christie's, London, 7 July 2005, lot 420) (Pl 5). It is no coincidence either that the scale and dimensions of Hogarth's *John Ranby* are so close to those of these busts by Rysbrack: he would have been at pains to make it so. Hogarth's canvas is nearly identical in height to *Edward Salter* and *John Barnerd* when their socles are included (although that on *Barnerd* is not original).

There were several reasons for Hogarth's provoking such aesthetic comparisons, but an

6 *Captain Thomas Coram* by James
McCardell after Hogarth
Engraving published 17 October 1739
Private collection

7 *Captain Coram*, 1740
Oil on canvas, 238.8 x 147.3 cm
Foundling Museum

especially significant one was his decision to participate in the aesthetic concerns that had occupied artist and theoreticians in Europe at least since the early years of the Renaissance in Italy. Hogarth's own *Analysis of Beauty* (1753) reveals that he was anxious to assert, as a prime mover in the conscious establishment of a distinctive British school of painting for the first time, that both he and it should be considered in a European context; and one of the most enduring controversies in European art had been the essentially irresolvable discussion as to which was superior, painting or sculpture, the *paragone*.

One of Hogarth's European contemporaries with whom he explicitly sympathised was the great French painter Jean-Baptiste Chardin, whose studio he suggested Philip Yorke and Daniel Wray should visit on a trip to Paris in 1749.[3] Other than Hogarth, there is no eighteenth-century painter who shows such an extraordinary sympathy for children as Chardin. Both artists avoid showing them as 'manikins', miniature adults togged out in scaled-down versions of adult dress, as had often been the way in earlier times, although Hogarth sometimes does so for satirical purposes (Pl 10). Instead, Chardin and Hogarth show children as

8 *La petite fille aux cérises*, 1738
Engraving by Charles-Nicolas Cochin *père* (1688-1754) after
Chardin
British Museum

9 'Second Stage of Cruelty', *Four Stages of Cruelty*, 1751
Engraving
British Museum

10 'Noon' in *The Four Times of the Day*

children, dressed as children, absorbed in childlike pursuits (Pl 8). Verses beneath Chardin's
La petite fille aux cérises of 1738 tell as much, implying that, naturally, this cannot last:

> Simple dans mes plaisirs, en ma colation,
> Je sçais trouver aussy, ma recreation

The self-absorption of childhood is related to Locke's analysis of childhood as a state in which the
individual is, morally speaking, a *tabula rasa*, a perception which led him to advocate the distinctive and specialized treatment of them.[4] Hogarth's *Grey children* is extraordinary in its depiction
of an inherent dichotomy: the cruelty that, unconsciously, children can inflict on other sentient
beings, yet which is entirely natural. *The Graham children* (Pl 11) contains elements of this kind,
in the teasing way in which the elder girl holds the cherries out of reach of the baby. Hogarth, however, is careful to contrast unconscious, strictly childish, cruelty of this kind with, say, the knowing

11 *The Graham children*, 1742
Oil on canvas, 160.5 x 181 cm
National Gallery, London

and deliberate torturing of a dog by Tom Nero in the first scene of *Four Stages of Cruelty*, a rather close contrast with the activity in *The Grey children*, and itself at the start of a narrative deriven by an unprecedented public assertion of the significance of cruelty to animals. Nero carries out this act of torture at a time when he is 'old enough to know better' or perhaps, more decisively, is at a stage of his development which, if he fails swiftly to receive moral instruction about right and wrong, will inevitably lead on to a life of moral inadequacy revealed in ever-increasing manifestations of cruelty. Nero never receives correction and so, in the second scene (Pl 9), he is seen mercilessly beating now, not a dog, but a horse; and so on, in the remaining scenes, to the murder of his mistress and his own execution. As both horrifically realistic and symbolic climax, the scientific dissection of his corpse in the fourth scene is a depiction of scientific examination of the purely physical that embodies – or implies – the moral analysis of the series.

12 *The five children of Charles I*
Seventeenth-century (?) copy of the paint-
ing by Anthony Van Dyck
Private collection

13 *Study of hands* by Nicolas Largillière
(1656-1746), *c.*1715
Oil on canvas, 65 x 53 cm
Musée du Louvre, Paris

14 *Sheet of eight heads* by Antoine Watteau
(1684-1721), *c.*1716
Chalks, 26.7 x 39.7 cm
Musée du Louvre, Paris

The theme of the passage of time to which Chardin's images of childhood so subtly allude
pervades what is Hogarth's greatest single painting devoted to infancy, *The Graham
Children* of 1742 (Pl 11), a picture in which the influence of Chardin has quite rightly been
noted.[5] The hints of mortality present in the picture are suggestive of the transience of childhood and of life itself, although this is a clumsy way of putting what Hogarth expresses with
the most delicate touch. They include the figure of Time, curiously represented by a child
cupid, with scythe and hourglass, surmounting a clock, a device 'without parallel in the history of clock ornamentation'.[6] While the picture was under way, the youngest child died, and
the familiar motif of a bird on the dead infant's chariot is portrayed by Hogarth as a dove with
its wings spread, suggestive of the flight of the soul, but so natural a detail in this context as

15 *Heads of his six servants, c.*1750-5
Oil on canvas, 63 x 75.5 cm
Tate, London, 2006

to operate almost subliminally; and the same is true of the carnations at the child's feet, with their stems crossed, symbolizing that life is 'a flower that soon fadeth', yet quite naturally lying next to the elaborate still life in the de Lamerie-style silver basket.[7]

Hogarth was very much aware of one of the few Old Masters whose sympathetic understanding of children approached his own: Anthony van Dyck. Indeed, Hogarth's shop sign at his sudio in Leicester Fields (now Leicester Square) was the 'Golden Head', an effigy of Van Dyck made out of cork by himself, and gilded. *The Graham children* is very much an 'imitation', in the contemporary Augustan sense, of Van Dyck's *The five children of Charles I* (Pl 12). Hogarth's reasons were not entirely theoretical or aesthetic. His own own patron, Daniel Graham, not only lived in Pall Mall, close to the Court (in a house he had just built in 1741), he also occupied the important position within the Court of Royal Apothecary, in which profession he was possessed of legendary skill. The 'modern' imitation of an 'ancient' model in this case is quite extreme, in view of the gulf that stretched between the respective social ranks of the sitters in the two portraits – from royal and bourgeois families respectively – and the transmutation of the courtly setting of the one into the *haut bourgeois* interior of the other. The brilliant handling of paint in both pictures is a key point of comparison, while Hogarth also picks up the way in which Van Dyck plays off the childishness of his subjects against the formality of the behaviour that they seek to adopt and which was expected of them. Van Dyck's presentation of the children, indeed, could hardly have been nore unlike that usual among his fellow-painters of the seventeenth century: he treats them with respect, of course, but also with humour that makes gentle fun both of the highly formalised genre of royal portraiture and of the elaborate court etiquette to which children belonging to it, as much as adults, had to conform. The humour of Van Dyck's picturederives in part from the fact that the young Charles is adopting the pose of Henry VII in Holbein's famous mural of the Tudor dynasty (then still on view in Whitehall Palace) but has to make an obvious effort to place his arm high enough in order to do do,and that his arm is supported by a St Bernard dog as large as he is. Meanwhile, the courtly props of table, ewer, column and drapes –tower over the children.

Hogarth brought a similar commingling of objective observation and compassion to the wholly exceptional *Heads of his six servants* (Pl 15) which is partly a variation upon the ancient theme of the Ages of Man in the case of the males present, from boyhood to old age. It is also surely, a deliberate transformation of the familiar French academic practice of making studies of heads from various angles within the compass of one sheet of paper, an exercise most common in the work of Watteau, who had a marked influence upon Hogarth, and which he had brought to a level of great sophistication (Pl 14). A related exercise was one in which other individual parts of the body, such as hands, might be observed with the same detachment yet, on occasion, fully painted with elaborate finish, and in the most complex arrangement, as in Largilliere's *Study of hands* (Pl 13). Hogarth takes this format out of the academy and the studio, drags it from the wings, as it were, to centre stage, and, in *Heads of his six servants* forces us to contemplate with a consciousness of shared humanity what would now be termed the 'marginalized' of society. It is this rare capacity for human sympathy that made Hogarth the great artist he was, and, as his work for the Foundling demonstrates, an equally remarkable human being.

1 Katharine Eustace, 'The key is Locke: Hogarth, Rysbrack and the Foundling Hospital', *The British Art Journal*, VII, 2 (Autumn 2006), pp. 34-49.
2 These subjects are treated in more detail in Robin Simon, *Hogarth, France and British Art. The rise of the arts in eighteenth-century Britain*, London, 2007 (=Simon), ch. 8.
3 See Simon, ch. 1.
4 Eustace, op. cit.
5 Judy Egerton, National Gallery Catalogues, *The British School*, London, 1998, pp. 134-45.
6 Ibid.
7 Ibid.

IV

'That Wondrous Child'
William Crotch, the musical phenomenon

JANET SNOWMAN

Sweet o'er my bosom stole the breath of fame
In early life, on Fancy's pinions borne
Infancy, Hugh Downman, 1775[1]

The Foundling Hospital was established at a time when attitudes towards children were changing throughout British society, a transformation that continued in the second half of the eighteenth century. The astonishing performances in London of the child phenomenon Wolfgang Amadeus Mozart in 1764-5 seemed to confirm the idea that children deserved to be taken far more seriously than had been conceivable in earlier times. The shadow of that great 'English' composer, George Frederic Handel, who had been so closely associated with the Foundling Hospital, continued to hang over British music, and the search for an 'English Mozart' was on. The remarkable child musician William Crotch (1775-1847) seemed to fit the bill...

1 *William Crotch* by James Fittler (1758-1835), published 12 May 1779 by Mrs Crotch, near St James's Street, Piccadilly. Engraving 32.5 x 23 cm. Private collection

After Henry Purcell's death in 1695, there was observed to be a long dark absence of 'English musical genius', which was to last well over a century.[2] London, the major musical capital in Europe, had thrived on entertainment by local and especially foreign musicians, but English composition was considered a failure. It was against this background that in 1770 Daines Barrington, the English lawyer and writer on music, published his influential report, *An account of a very remarkable young Musician*, recording his examination of the eight-year-old Mozart when in London with his family (April 1764-July 1765). Barrington's 'testing' of the young prodigy was interrupted by Mozart's having run away to play with a cat, and to trot around the room on a hobby horse – alongside the scientific enquiry, childish concerns did not go unmentioned.[3] The search for a British Mozart coincided with changes in social and familial attitudes towards childhood, at a time of growing national identity and in a period promoting the cult of celebrity, a fashion much

2 *William Crotch*
by Sir William Beechey
(1753-1839), 1786.
Oil on canvas, 127 x 110 cm.
Royal Academy of Music, London

3 *The Musical Phaenomenon* by ?
'Mr Harrington',
published in the *London Magazine*,
April 1779, and sold separately.
Engraving 16 x 9 cm.
Private collection

equalled in our own times. Such a saviour of native music appeared to have arrived with the discovery of the English musical prodigy and artist, William Crotch, who was immortalized in a superb canvas by William Beechey (Pl 2), a 'celebrity portrait' if ever there was one. Much, however, can also be learned from the contemporary press and popular engravings, and here I will consider three prints relating to this 'musical phaenomenon'.

In 1778, at the age of three, William was hailed as a true child of nature, untutored and naturally gifted. The writer and musician Charles Burney noted, following a visit to the child's Norwich home, that William:

> ... played entirely by ear, could transpose into any key whatever he played when a little over two... his appearance and manners are those of a mere child, but his mind is in general intelligent and quick beyond his years.[4]

A portrait of the child by James Fittler (Pl 1), later marine engraver to George III, shows one of the earlier images of a British 'celebrity' – certainly the youngest – engraved to a commission from Mrs Crotch and dedicated to Sir Harbord Harbord, the local Norwich MP. The child is seen full face on in his fancy hat, and the viewer is forced to engage directly with the young, innocent baby, with his simple round cheeks, large eyes and pointed chin, all characteristics of babyhood shared, to take a famous example with which this composition bears comparison, with Holbein's portrait of the infant Edward VI, also in his fancy hat, though with his eyes cast down, holding a teething rattle like a sceptre (1539, National Gallery of Art, Washington).

A report in *the Norwich Mercury* a few months earlier had described William as 'still sucking'.[5] Here he could be said to exemplify Hogarth's comments on the visual characteristics of the young infant with its 'unmeaning stare', though without the 'open mouth and simple grin'.[6] The two portraits, William's with his arms firmly closed, also share the idea of an inscriptive panel, though the framing device used for William, the son of a carpenter, comprising a laureated roundel with a chiselled stone plinth, also brings to mind Hogarth's portraits of, for example, the children Hannah (*c*1748-50) and George Osborne (*c*1750), with their own sculptural settings. The idea of casting the infant William in monumental stone as a British icon perhaps acts as a way for the parents

The Musical Phænomenon.

to capture and preserve, with pride, as Hogarth would describe (writing of the face), 'from infancy till the body has done growing, the contents both of the body and the face, and every part of their surface' which, Hogarth notes, 'are daily changing into more variety, till they obtain a certain medium'.[7]

The monument here captures the genius of a long-awaited gifted child of British composition, who could perhaps deliver British music from the doldrums. This idea is reflected in the musical trophies to the right, which include a sunburst flower-like Apollonian face on a lyre, similar to that carved on Roubiliac's statue of Handel (*Victoria and Albert Museum*). Handel had been perceived by some as an honorary and true Englishman, partly through his association with the works of those literary heroes, the poets Dryden, Milton and Pope.[8] With an organ to the right, a flourish of curtain on the left and a roll of manuscript with fictive music threaded onto his arm – the notation is 'in the style of Handel' – the print is also important because it is the first to allude to the child's perceived equal artistic ability, in particular his love of drawing boats and windmills; parental involvement again shows itself here, and the print would have also functioned as today's family photograph.

The growing commercial magazine press, often aimed at women, in particular clamoured for biographical material illustrative of celebrity and with portraits which could also be purchased separately, with differently priced printed editions. A puff for William Crotch's 'likeness for sale' (Pl 3) in the *St James's Chronicle*, Tuesday 30 March 1779, is described as:

The Musical Phaenomenon, being a most accurate and striking likeness of that extraordinary Genius, Master W. Crotch (in shade 2s 6d, etching 1s 6d) taken from life by Mr Harrington, No 62 South Molton Street.

The same advertisement appeared alongside an article on the child in the *London Magazine* of April 1779. Prints were also used as concert advertisements, sold ahead of the William's visits to various towns during his gruelling tours throughout Britain, where he was paraded by his mother at a fee of 2s, as demonstrated on the promotional handbill titled *The Astonishing Musical Infant* (Pl 4).

A passage in the *London Magazine* describes how William was displayed at 'three years and eight months at Mrs Hart's, Milliner, Piccadilly, every day between 1-3 in publick'.[9]

> A large organ is placed upon the centre of the room, against the wainscot; it is raised upon a stage about two feet from the floor, and a semicircular iron rod is fixed to it as to secure him in his seat and separates him from the company. An arm chair is placed upon this stage, and in it a common very small matted chair which his mother fastens behind with a handkerchief to the other, that he may not fall out, for he is a wanton, and full of antick tricks in the short intervals from playing. A book is placed before him, as it was a musick book, and strangers in a distant part of the room may mistake it for such; but it is no more than a magazine or some other pamphlet with an engraved frontispiece; this he looks at and emotes himself with the figures in the plate, while he is playing any tune, or striking into his own harmony. In short, he laughs, prattles and looks about at the company, at the same time keeping his little hands employed on the keys, and playing with so much unconcern that you would be tempted to think he did but know what he was doing. He appears to be fondest of solemn basses, and church music, particularly the 104th psalm. As soon as he has finished a regular tune, or part of a tune, or played some little fancy notes of his own, he flops and has the pranks of a wanton boy; some of the company then generally give him a cake, an apple or an orange, to induce him to play again … unless you touch the pride of his little heart by telling him he has forgot such a tune, or he cannot play it, this seldom fails of producing the effect and he is sure to play it with additional spirit. After playing more than an hour, he desired to be taken down, and to have a piece of chalk, he then entertained himself and the company with drawing outlines on the floor ….

To John Locke, music was thought to have been a diversion from greater responsibilities, with its practice retained by the upper class within private quarters,[10] ideas given recent expression in Jamila Gavin's recent novel and (adapted) play *Coram Boy*.[11] To portray a male child with a musical instrument was most unusual, as this undermined current conceptions of male-ness.[12] Locke's view that music 'wastes so much of a young Man's time, to gain but a moderate Skill in it; and engages often in such odd Company' was a feeling applied to the fine arts in general, especially in the later 18th century, and was expressed through worries about effeminacy and sensibility.[13] Jean-Jacques Rousseau's *Emile* (1762, translated into English in 1763), promoted the author's ideal education for a young boy where learning is achieved by continually discovering works of nature, and was evocative of Enlightenment attitudes to the individual as a reasoning human being.[14] In his published report on Crotch to the Royal Society, Burney, writing in 1779, showed his own awareness of these values and concern for William's infant well-being:

4 Promotional handbill, Newcastle, 1780

5 *William Crotch* by John Sanders
(1750-1825), 1778.
Oil on canvas, 95 x 74 cm. Royal
Academy of Music, London

… nor does he, as yet, seem a subject for instruction; for till his reason is sufficiently mature to comprehend and retain the precepts of a master and something like a wish for information appears, by a ready and willing obedience to his injunctions, trammels of rules would but disgust and if forced upon him, destroy the miraculous parts of his self-taught instruction' … it must not be forgotten that this child is equally delighted with drawing as with music.[15]

William Crotch is shown again in an image that is reflective of Rousseau's literary ideas: a child unbound, unswaddled and free of constraints, free-thinking, and using his intellect and imagination to discover a new skill for himself. This is an aquatint by John Sanders (Pl 5, published 1781), showing the child with bare feet, upright on a neo-classical stool, wearing a flowing muslin dress, apparently looking at the Muse for approval, as she ticks off his accomplishment in the form of Handel's 'Lessons'. William is depicted with a sense of *jeu d'esprit*, but is also concentrating on his learning and achieving. Again, his drawing books lie on the floor. Rousseau in *Émile* writes:

Before the child is enslaved by our prejudices his first wish is always to be free and comfortable. The plainest and most comfortable clothes, those which leave him most liberty, are what he always likes best.[16]

While Locke's ideas on keeping children's feet wet and cold may appear strange to us,[17] Rousseau also thought going barefoot was good for the spirit, and made for a happy and free child, allowing genius and creativity to flourish. The Exeter-based doctor and poet Hugh Downman reiterated these thoughts on freedom of limb for a female child in his long and passionate poem, *Infancy*, lines from which are quoted at the end of this chapter.[18]

Two lines of poetry engraved beneath the print come from Joseph Warton's newly published (1780) poem *Ode to Fancy*: 'Lovely Muse, Thy spirit o'er my soul diffuse, O'er all my artless songs preside.'[19] The iconography shows the Muse with her lyre and caduceus, as the personification of the poetic imagination (see lines 9-13 below), with Pegasus here representing the incarnation of poetic inspiration:

> O Nymph with loosely-flowing hair
> With buskin'd leg, and bosom bare
> Thy waist with myrtle-girdle bound
> Thy brows with Indian feathers crown'd
> Waving in thy snowy hand
> An all-commanding magic wand.

Fancy (Imagination) is evoked at different stages in the poem, and the word 'artless' as used here implies Nature, or without artifice. A banderole holds the word 'SUADERE' (to please, to persuade, perhaps implying 'to reason'), and the verse permits a linking of the image of William with British poetics and literary ideas of Enlightenment as related to imagination, natural genius and reason, expressed pictorially alongside those espoused by Rousseau in *Émile*. On the death of Alexander Pope (1744), Warton had suggested that poetry should turn away from the fashion of moralising and should instead emphasise invention and imagination.[20] In his *Ode to Fancy*, he pleaded for a warm, enthusiastic, and rapturous divine energy as a validation of the individual's right to be emotional.[21] Perhaps the addition of this text to the print had been suggested by Burney, by the organist and artist William Jackson, or by the Revd Alexander Schomberg, three individuals in the background of William Crotch's early years. William's appearance in this print, in an unbreeched state at the age of six, little different indeed from his appearance at an even younger age (Pl 5), may have been encouraged by his mother, as a way of suggesting in a circulating print the idea of his being younger than he was, for promotional reasons.

Such prints as these conveyed great expectations of William's young life, but his compositional skills caused ultimate disappointment to his supporters when, by the age of ten, he had not so far lived up to the conception of him as another infant Mozart, a god-given child, representative of the Enlightenment.[22] For William, as for other infant prodigies of the period, the breath of fame more often turned into an ill wind. In fact, William was regularly ill, having followed a treacherous life of appearances throughout Britain, on journeys fraught with coach crashes, poor roads, unsafe inns and other hazards; and the *Gentleman's Magazine* in July 1781 even mistakenly announced William's death, at the age of six, from an accident. In 1832 he wrote:

6 *William Crotch*
by John Sanders (1750-1825),
published 6 August 1782 after a
painting of July 1781 (now lost).
Aquatint, 36 x 27 cm.
Private collection

I look back on this part of my life with
pain and humiliation, but I desire
most gratefully to acknowledge the
Almighty hand of Divine Providence
which brought so much good out of
evil.[23]

This speaks its own tale of manipulation, from which the small child had no escape.

Ultimately, Crotch's career was a distinguished one. He was appointed professor of music at Oxford at the age of 22, and in 1822 became the first Principal of the Royal Academy of Music. He was greatly influenced by the *Discourses* of Sir Joshua Reynolds, and based the first British public lectures on music upon Reynolds' ideas. He is attributed with writing the chimes in 1793 for Great St Mary's, Cambridge, a pattern of notes later adapted for Big Ben in Westminster: they were actually based on bars from the introductory passages to Handel's 'I know that My Redeemer Liveth' (*Messiah*). Handel was himself a Governor and benefactor of the Foundling Hospital, and in his Will bequeathed to the Hospital a fair copy of *Messiah*. He established a musical tradition which has continued to the present day through Coram Family's Handel Concert held each February to celebrate his birthday.

Crotch himself, as noted above, possessed real gifts as an artist, and his drawings and watercolours are represented in many major British collections. His friend John Constable is said to have been influenced by Crotch in applying the date and time of day to his landscape studies. 'His friend John Constable is said to have been influenced by Crotch in applying the date and time of day to his landscape studies. Pencil portraits by Constable of Crotch and his infant daughter, Isabel, when asleep, are pasted into Crotch's 'Memoirs'.

1 Hugh Downman, *Infancy or the management of children: a poem in three books* (Edinburgh,1776), 6th edn, Exeter, 1803, Book IV, p91, ll 11-12.

2 AV Beedell, *The Decline of the English Musician 1788-1888: a family of English musicians in Ireland, England, Mauritius and Australia*, Oxford, 1992, p41. Also Deborah Rohr, *The Careers of British Musicians 1750-1850 A profession of artisans*, Cambridge, 2001. Lack of direct patronage of professional British musicians by the aristocracy differed markedly from the situation in Europe: Beedell, p50.

3 Daines Barrington FRS. 'Account of a very remarkable young musician', *Philosophical Transactions of the Royal Society*, vol 60 (December 1770), p54, XIII.

4 Charles Burney, *An account of the infant musician William Crotch*, read at the Royal Society, 18 February 1779; published in both *Philosophical Transactions*, pp183-206, p193. Published also in the *Annual Register* the same year; slightly altered shorter version published in the *Gentleman's Magazine* and also as a separate volume. Reproduced again in the *Norwich Mercury*, 15 January 1780. Burney, on his return from his European tour in 1770, had been concerned with finding a way to provide a formal course of training for British musicians, with native British teachers, based on the idea of the *ospedale* in Italy, in particular that in Naples.

5 *Norwich Mercury*, 25 April 1778.

6 William Hogarth, *The Analysis of, Beauty*, http://www.tristramshandyweb.it/e-texts/hogarth/analysis_html/title-page.htm, accessed 3 September 2006. Chapter XV 'Of the Face', pp129-30.

7 Hogarth, *The Analysis of Beauty*, p132.

8 Suzanne Aspden, 'Fam'd Handel Breathing', *Journal of the American Musicological Society*, vol 55, no. 1 (Spring 2002), pp39-90.

9 Anon, 'The Musical Phaenomenon', *London Magazine*, London, April 1779. Similar descriptive puffs on her precocity were used to describe the Welsh prodigy, Elizabeth Randles, said at the age of 16 months as showing 'strong musical powers'. She first performed in public in 1802, with 'an apple on her right side and a cake on her left, both of which she was to receive if she played well': John S Sainsbury, ed, *Dictionary of Musicians from the earliest ages to the present time comprising the most important biographical contents* (London, 1825, vol II), facsimile reprint, Da Capo Press, New York, 1966, p334. She was painted twice by John Downman, and was also the subject of an engraving by the Welsh landscape artist Moses Griffiths.

10 Richard Leppert, *Music and Image* (Cambridge, 1988), 1993, p24.

11 Jamila Gavin, *Coram Boy*, London, 2000. Adapted for the Royal National Theatre by Helen Edmundson. First performance 5 November 2005.

12 Four painted portraits of William Crotch, two at the Royal Academy of Music (by William Beechey and John Sanders), show him depicted with cello, keyboard and/or violin.

13 Margaret JM Ezell, 'John Locke's Images of Childhood: early eighteenth century response *to Some Thoughts Concerning Education*', *Eighteenth-century Studies*, vol 17, no. 2 (Winter 1983), p10.

14 Jean-Jacques Rousseau, *Émile*. http://www.ilt.columbia.edu/pedagogies/rousseau/contents2.html (International Learning Technologist, Columbia University), accessed 4 July 2007 (Book I – [258:]).

15 *Norwich Mercury, 1780 (Burney)*.

16 Rousseau quoted in Jane Ashelford, *The Art of Dress: Clothes and Society 1500-1914*. London, 1996, p279.

17 John Locke, *Some Thoughts Concerning Education*. www.fordham.edu/halsall/mod/1692locke-education.html. Section 7 (p5/102). Accessed 4 July 2007.

18 Hugh Downman in *Infancy* writes 'Let then the sturdy boy unlimited/Follow the bent of nature; nor too soon/Enslave thy daughter: let her limbs possess/Their utmost freedom to the extremest verge/Which custom will permit (p142).

19 See Joseph Warton, *Ode to Fancy*. Representative Poetry on-line, University of Toronto, Canada - http://rpo.library.utoronto.ca/poem/2259.html.

20 Benjamin Boyce, 'Sounding Shells and Little Prattlers in the mid-Eighteenth Century English Ode', *Eighteenth-century Studies*, vol 8, no. 3 (Spring 1975), pp245-64.

21 Professor Murray Roston, personal communication, 2007.

22 For examples of Crotch's childish works, see MS5295, Music book containing two musical productions composed by William Crotch at the ages of 8 and 9 (*Hirlais Owain* or *The Drinking Horn of Owen* (1784) and *Gwin, King of Norway* (1785). And MS5293, Child's notebook, signed by William Crotch, with transcriptions of work by various composers, including some of his own when a child, Cambridge 1786. Both Norfolk Record Office, Norwich. A sales catalogue from Ellis and Company, published in London in 1896 by Leonard Smithers, shows an entry for 'Two Favourite Sonatas. Dedicated by permission to Dr Burney. Holland & Co (*c.*1786). Folio, engraved list of subscribers, the music engraved'. Inscribed in a boyish hand 'Master Crotch begs Mr Beechey's acceptance of these Sonatas'. The catalogue records: 'This is probably the earliest and rarest publication of the juvenile prodigy.'

23 MS11244. Memoirs compiled by William Crotch from his own and 200 family letters, 1777-1832. Norfolk Records Office, Norwich, Note on Summer, 1780.

V

Catalogue

KATHERINE FIELD

A PERSPECTIVE VIEW OF THE FOUNDLING HOSPITAL, WITH EMBLEMATIC FIGURES.

Myriads of Proselites sustain thy Cause!
Throng to thy Altars and obey thy Laws;
From hence, fair Venus, spring those sweet Supplys
To fill the Mansions which to thee arise!
To his Grace John Duke of Bedford, This Plate is humbly Inscribed

These Mansions raisd by Patrons kind & great,
Where Babes deserted find a safe Retreat.
Tho' Frenchmen sneer, their boasted first Design,
British Benevolence shall far outshine!
by his Graces most Dutiful and Obedient Servant Margrett Granville

CAT. 5 Charles Grignon & Pierre-Charles
Canot after Samuel Wale
Perspective View of the Foundling Hospital, 1749
Engraving
Foundling Museum

The works in this catalogue are by William Hogarth
(1697-1764) unless otherwise stated

1 *George Osbourne, later John Ranby, Jnr,* 1748-50
Oil on canvas, 81.28 x 73.7 cm
Tate. Presented by Mrs Gilbert Cousland 1996
to celebrate the Tate Gallery Centenary and the Hogarth Tercentenary 1997

2 *Hannah, daughter of John Ranby, Snr,* 1748-50
Oil on canvas, 81.28 x 73.7 cm
Tate. Presented by Mrs Gilbert Cousland 1996
to celebrate the Tate Gallery Centenary and the Hogarth Tercentenary 1997

Hannah and George Osborne, aged here about nine and six, were the illegitimate children of Dr John Ranby, Principal Serjeant-Surgeon to George II, and a friend and neighbour of Hogarth in Chiswick. Their mother, whom Ranby had never married, had died in 1746, creating a rather unconventional household. George was brought up as Ranby's heir and changed his name to John Ranby by royal licence in 1756. Hannah is not mentioned in her father's will of 1773, indicating that she may have already died by that date. She is known to have married a Walter Waring and had two children, Walter, who is identified as attending Eton, and Elizabeth.

Hannah and George are representative of what the Foundling Hospital was trying to achieve by preserving young lives. In the eyes of Thomas Coram and the Foundling Governors, illegitimacy did not scar a child's character irreparably and they could be brought up virtuously and given skills so as to become contributing members of society.

3 *Martin Folkes,* 1741
Oil on canvas. 76.2 x 63.5 cm
Royal Society, London

Martin Folkes (1690-1754) was, with John Milner, the first Vice-President of the Board of Governors of the Foundling Hospital. He was present with Hogarth, Captain Coram, the Duke of Richmond and Theodore Jacobson as the first children were accepted into the Hospital. As the picture dates from 1741 it seems likely that it was commissioned to celebrate Folkes' becoming president of the Royal Society in that year.

A man of independent means, Folkes was able to devote himself to antiquarian studies and natural philosophy. The seriousness of his studies becomes apparent in the three auction sales after his death. The sale of his library alone was made up of 5,122 lots and took place over forty continuous days (Sundays excepted) beginning 2 February 1756. He also seems to have been an admirer of Hogarth's prints, as two collections of them appear in the catalogue for the sale of his prints and drawings 15 January 1756. He was proposed as a fellow of the Royal Society in 1713 and by 1723 was elected vice-president under then president Sir Isaac Newton. Folkes later presented this portrait to the Royal Society, together with portraits of Isaac Newton by John Vanderbank and Francis Bacon by Paul van Somer.

CAT. 3 *Martin Folkes*, 1741
Oil on canvas. 76.2 x 63.5 cm
Royal Society, London

4 *Christ and the Apostles*, 1744
Ink and bluish wash on paper, 17.8 x 20.3 cm
© Royal London Hospital Archives
Courtesy of Royal London Hospital Archives

The London Hospital was founded in 1740 on the same principles as the Foundling Hospital in that it was paid for not by the church or state but through benefactions and voluntary subscriptions. This drawing was given by Hogarth and it was subsequently engraved and used by the Hospital for various purposes throughout the 18th century. The scene depicts Christ and his disciples observing the sick being transported to the entrance of an antique building which represented the hospital. The caption, in Hogarth's hand, reads '*In as much as ye have done it unto one of the least of these my Brethren, ye have done it unto me. St Matt. XXV .v. 40*'.

The drawing is mentioned as a gift from the artist in the House Committee's report to the Court of Governors on 22 June 1744. Its first use appears to have been as the head-piece for a publicity sheet published in 1745, to raise funds and awareness of the Hospital, much as Hogarth's headpiece for the Foundling Hospital was used.

5 Charles Grignon & Pierre-Charles Canot after Samuel Wale
Perspective View of the Foundling Hospital, 1749
Engraving
Foundling Museum

Until the age of between three and five the Foundling children were sent out to wet-nurses in the country and watched over by the appointed inspector for that area. When the children returned to London, they wore the Hospital's uniform which Hogarth had designed between 1745 and 1746, which can be seen on the children at the centre of the print. A contemporary description describes them thus:

> The Boys have only one garment which is made jacket fashion, of Yorkshire serge with a slip of red clothe cross their shoulder; their shirts lapping over their Collar resembling a cape; their breeches hang loose a great way down their legs, instead of buttons is a slip of red cloth furbelowed. The Girls Petticoats are also of Yorkshire Serge; and their stays are covered with the same, of which a slip turns back over their shoulders, like that of the boys, and is of the same colour. Their buff bib and apron are linen, the shift is gathered and drawn with bobbins, in the manner of a close tucker. The Boys and Girls hats are white, and tied round with red binding.

Apart from a decision to provide a new style of bodice for the girls in 1760, the uniform underwent very few changes over the course of a century.

6 *Self-portrait painting the Comic Muse*, 1764
Etching and engraving
Andrew Edmunds

Hogarth's ability to record the harsh realities of London's streets must in part derive from his own childhood experiences. He was born on 10 November 1697 as the fifth child of Richard Hogarth and his wife Anne. All but one of the four eldest children were already

Self-portrait painting the Comic Muse, 1758

dead at his birth and three younger siblings were also die, two during their father's impris-
onment for debt.

    This self-portrait makes reference to Hogarth having been appointed 'Serjeant Painter of
all his Majesty's works, as well belonging to his Royal Palaces or houses, as to his great
Wardrobe or otherwise', on 6 June 1757. The exhibited version of the print, dating from the
year of Hogarth's death, differs from that illustrated above: Hogarth has obliterated his official title with hatching. While it has been suggested that the print is simply under revision,
this curious procedure is more likely to have been the result of the pessimism that afflicted

Hogarth late in his career. He may well have come to reflect upon the somewhat hollow nature of his official title, while this composition was being used as the frontispiece in folios of his prints sold to the public. While the position of Serjeant Painter was financially rewarding, it did little for Hogarth's reputation as an artist, and was not connected with securing any major royal commissions for paintings: the duties largely involved overseeing the decorations of the royal palaces. Hogarth had striven to gain royal commissions earlier in his career but had been thwarted by those who favoured the painter and architect William Kent. Hogarth had actually been forcibly removed from the Chapel Royal while carrying out preliminary sketches for his proposed picture of the wedding of the Prince of Orange to the Princess Royal in 1733.

The position of Sergeant Painter came with a notional annual salary of £10, which was rather less than that of, for example, John Gower, Rat-killer to the King, at £48 3s 4d. None the less, Hogarth's true salary was much more than that, because the position came with a monopoly on the painting and gilding of all the royal palaces and conveyances, including banners and tents for royal troops and ships. After paying his deputy, who supervised the completion of the work, his salary would certainly have allowed him to live comfortably, and in 1763 alone Hogarth is known to have made £120 clear of expenses from this lucrative sinecure.

7 'View of Ranby's House, Chiswick, from Hogarth's Villa' (opposite)
Etching
Andrew Edmunds

This etching is, in fact, variously described, on the one hand (as here) as showing the view across the fields from Hogarth's own country house in Chiswick towards that of his friend John Ranby, but elsewhere as showing Hogarth's own house. As Val Bott convincingly demonstrates (*The British Art Journal*, VIII, 1, forthcoming), there can be no doubt that it is Hogarth's house that is depicted, specifically, the second house from the left, complete with its distinctive boundary wall that also survives, now running alongside the dual carriageway towards the west after the 'Hogarth Roundabout'. Hogarth's own marriage was childless, but we know that he and his wife were responsible for a number of Foundling children from 1756. After Hogarth's death, Jane Hogarth wrote to the Hospital to allow the children they had in their care to remain so that they might enjoy a summer in countryside, playing in the fields here depicted. One of her letters, of 28 June 1765, reads:

> ... imagining that if the Children which are under my inspection was Brought to the House when the Year was expired which is but a few months to come; it would be but a trifling Expence to the House; but perhaps a Material Difference to the Children as they would enjoy the Benefit of a Run in the Country for the Summer Season, which in all probability would quite establish their Healths.

8 Ravenet and Picot after William Hogarth, *The Pool of Bethesda*, 1772
Engraving
Andrew Edmunds

This scene of Christ miraculously healing the sick was part of Hogarth's scheme for the decoration of the Grand Staircase of St Bartholomew's Hospital and his first attempt at history

a View of Mr Ranby the Surgeon's house. Taken from Hogarth's window at Chiswick

painting on a grand scale. The subject-matter is known to have been used in other painted works for hospitals in Europe, including Murillo's *Pool of Bethesda* completed for the Church of the Caridad (Charity) in Seville and now in the National Gallery, London. The picture was hung upon the wall on 7 April 1736 and on 12 April the Hospital announced in the *London Evening Post*:

> The ingenious Mr Hogarth, one of the Governors of St Bartholomew's Hospital, has presented to the said Hospital a very fine Piece of Painting representing the miracle wrought by our Saviour at the Pool of Bethesda, which was hung up in their great stair-case last Wednesday.

9 Ravenet and Delatre after William Hogarth, *The Good Samaritan,* 1772
Engraving
Andrew Edmunds

Hogarth wrested the commission for the St Bartholomew's pictures from the grasp of the Italian painter Jacopo Amigoni in February 1734, by offering to complete the work free of charge. This led to his being elected a governor of the Hospital in July the same year. These machinations highlight Hogarth's lifelong struggle to gain patronage for English artists in the highly regarded field of history painting, which included pictures of religious of mytho-logical subject-matter. As he records in his autobiographical 'Anecdotes' (manuscript in the British Library) he was determined to succeed:

> … in what the puffers in books call the great style of History painting; so that without having had a stroke of this grand business before, I quitted small portraits and familiar conversations, and, with a smile at my own temerity, commenced history painter, and on a great staircase at St. Bartholomew's painted two Scripture stories… These I presented to the Charity, and thought they might serve as a specimen to shew that, were there an inclination in England for encouraging historical pictures, such a first essay might prove the painting them more easily attainable than is generally imagined.

The completion of the pictures in 1734-6 meant that examples of Hogarth's work as a history painter upon continental lines was on permanent public display in the centre of London, an extremely rare opportunity for English artists at that time.

10 *The Bruiser*, 1763
Etching and engraving
Andrew Edmunds

This print arose out of the dispute between Hogarth, the Revd Charles Churchill and John Wilkes, MP. Wilkes had attacked Hogarth in his radical weekly publication *The North Briton*, and had been further supported in his attack by his friend, Charles Churchill. Regardless of the fact that Churchill was a fellow governor of the Foundling Hospital (elected 27 December 1758), Hogarth proceeded to attack him in this print. Hogarth has re-used the plate from his *Self-portrait with pug* of 1745 and replaced his own image with that of Churchill in the guise of a drunken and slovenly black bear, in a torn clerical collar. Churchill's satire, *An Epistle to William Hogarth*, in which he presents the artist as being too ill and infirm to be given any credit, it being urinated upon by Hogarth's pug, the ever-loyal 'Trump'. Hogarth himself can be seen in the lower right corner, commanding a dancing bear and monkey, who are meant to represent Churchill and Wilkes.
The dispute was well documented in the press with numerous verses satirizing the situation including the following, published in both the *London Magazine* and the *St James' Chronicle*:

> The Painter smarts from Churchill's manly Line,
> And tit for tat, pays Poem with Design.
> Who's right, who's wrong, I neither know nor care;
> I read, I gaze, and so – fight Dog, fight Bear.

Horace Walpole echoed this opinion: '… never did two angry men of their abilities throw mud with less dexterity.' Hogarth did rather well financially from the argument. In his surviving manuscript notes he calculated that he made £4.2s from his print of Wilkes and a further £30.15s from *The Bruiser*.

11 *Martin Folkes*, 1742
Etching and engraving
Foundling Museum

A curious letter in the Royal Society archives reveals that Folkes had an interesting second career as a smuggler and merchant of condoms. The relevant letter, addressed to Folkes by John Burrows, and dated 3 December 1743, discusses the need for secrecy in his venture. As condoms were generally sold quite openly it seems that this may have been in order to protect Folkes' reputation. The following excerpt implies that he was something of an expert in his field:

> As you are a Wise Man & a Philosopher, as well as a C—m Merchant, you can tell whether these Goods are a perishable Commodity, or not: that is to say, whether they are subject to receive Damage by lying by. If they are, they must be used with Caution: For I have had 'em a long while in my Drawer.

above The Court Room, Foundling Hospital (Foundling Museum), with Hogarth's *Moses before Pharaoh's daughter* at the far end

CAT 10 *The Bruiser,* 1763
Etching and engraving

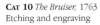

12 *Engraved plate for the print of Martin Folkes*
Copper
Andrew Edmunds

The copper plates created for making Hogarth's prints are quite rare survivals. We know from his will that Hogarth left his plates to his wife in order that she might continue to sell prints from them and so help to support herself after his death. After her death in 1789 they were sold to Joseph Boydell who used them to publish a folio of Hogarth's works. This plate, for his print after the portrait of Martin Folkes, survives in very good condition. Marks on the reverse show how Hogarth re-worked the plate and made corrections to his design.

13 *Moses brought before Pharaoh's Daughter*
Etching and engraving, 1752
Foundling Museum

This engraving is after the oil painting which Hogarth donated to the Hospital in 1746 to be displayed in the Court Room (see illustration above). This room is of immense importance to the history of British art as it constituted the first co-ordinated public display of the work of living artists. In addition to *Moses brought before Pharaoh's Daughter*, it was decorated with three religious works on the same scale and seven roundels depicting views of other London Hospitals, while the overmantel contained Rysbrack's marble relief.
The scene Hogarth has chosen is suggestive of the Foundling Hospital's working practice. Pharaoh's daughter, in an action symbolic of the Hospital's obligations, gently reaches out towards Moses, the first foundling, to bring him into her care. He has been brought into her presence by his wet-nurse, who can be seen being paid for her services, just as those in the employ of the Hospital would have been.

14 (right) After William Hogarth, *Unused ticket to a performance of Handel's Messiah*
Engraving printed in red ink
Andrew Edmunds

Hogarth's design for the Hospital's Coat of Arms (*c.* 1747) was used for a variety of purposes, including this, a ticket (unused) for a performance of Handel's *Messiah*. The first performance in England of this great oratorio took place in 1750 in the Foundling Hospital's new chapel, when it was personally overseen by Handel. The composer, himself a governor of the Hospital, continued to do soon annually, until ill health forced him to stop. These performances were of immense financial benefit to the charity, realising a total of around £7000.

15 After William Hogarth, engraved by F. Morellon La Cave, *The Foundlings*
Engraving
Foundling Museum

This print depicts Thomas Coram, founder of the Foundling Hospital, carrying the Hospital's Charter at the centre of the picture. He is engaged in rescuing a child from a distraught mother who had been about commit infanticide. Coram had begun his drive to establish the Hospital in about 1719 as a result of the abandoned infants he saw on London's streets and surrounding fields as he went about his daily business.
Hogarth has shown the Foundling children with implements of the skills which they were taught, in an effort to ensure that they could support themselves in later life. The Governors had determined that the children would:
> … learn to undergo with Contentment the most Servile and laborious Offices; for notwithstanding the innocence of the Children, yet as they are exposed and abandoned by their Parents, they ought to submit to the lowest stations, and should not be educated in such a manner as may put them upon a level with the Children of Parents who have the Humanity and Virtue to preserve them, and the Industry to Support them.

The girls are depicted with spinning wheels, samplers, rakes, and brooms, suited to their roles chiefly as housemaids, while the boys learn to make nets and pick oakum in preparation either for employment at sea or as agricultural labourers, occupations reflected in Michael Rysbrack's marble relief on the chimneypiece in the Court Room of the Hospital: *Charity children engaged in navigation and husbandry*, 1745. The children's apprenticeships to their trade were extraordinarily long: twenty-four years for the boys and twenty-one for the girls, in the hope that they might not return to a life of poverty. Hogarth's image was used by the Hospital as the headpiece for a letter appealing for subscriptions. It would have also have provided an opportunity for Hogarth to advertise himself, as it would have been sent to some of the richest and most influential people in the country.

16 J. McArdell after William Hogarth, *Daniel Lock*
Engraving
Andrew Edmunds

Hogarth named a child after Daniel Lock (1681-1754) in 1746, probably as a result of Lock's role in the foundation of a hospital of the same name, in which the poor were treated for venereal disease. The Lock Hospital was situated in Lanesborough House, Hyde Park Corner, now the site of the Lanesborough Hotel. Lock was elected a governor of the Foundling Hospital on 29 March 1749.

17 (above) After Louis-François Roubiliac (1695-1762). *Trump.* Second half of the 18th century. Marble, length 14 cm
The Hogarth Group

Perhaps because they were of similar appearance and temperament to himself, Hogarth owned several pug dogs. One of his later favourites, Trump, makes several more or less irreverent appearances: in *Self-portrait with pug*, 1745; the conversation piece *Captain Lord George Graham* in his cabin, *c.*1745; and in the print *The Bruiser*, 1763.
When Roubiliac sculpted his terracotta bust of Hogarth in 1741 (National Portrait Gallery) he completed an accompanying model of Trump at the same time. A plaster cast of the original was passed to the Chelsea porcelain factory for reproduction in the mid-1740s, while the Wedgwood factory also produced black basalt versions from 1774. The catalogue from Roubiliac's sale after his death in 1762 shows that he was selling plaster casts of 'A pug dog,' indicating that little Trump may have been quite a popular item to purchase.
Samuel Ireland, author of *Graphic Illustrations of Hogarth*, published in 1799, included an engraving of both sculptures together. He added:

I have introduced, beneath the bust, the figure of Hogarth's dog Trump, modelled by the same artist. It had been jocularly observed by him, that there was a close resemblance betwixt his own countenance and that of this favourite dog, who was his faithful friend, and companion for many years, and for whom he had conceived a greater share of attachment than is usually bestowed on these domestic animals. I make no apology for the introduction of his portrait to the notice of the reader, because the attentions, of which the master thought him worthy, have in a manner (if I may be allowed to say so much concerning a dog) conferred a sort of dignity upon his memory.'

18 English Delftware. *Hogarth's Punch Bowl*, 1730s
Foundling Museum

No doubt in acknowledgement of Hogarth's deep involvement with the Foundling Hospital, at some point it acquired his punchbowl. This piece of English delftware would have held a mixture of punch, from which drinkers could help themselves with the use of a ladle. One such bowl, with *chinoiserie* decoration, appears in one of Hogarth's most famous prints, *A Midnight Modern Conversation.* The dragon on the present piece copies those of late 17th- and early 18th-century Chinese porcelain, and was a design used by two early English porcelain factories, Worcester and Bow.

19 Register of children's names (19th-century copy)
London Metropolitan Archives

As each child was accepted it was baptised and given a new name by the governors of the Hospital and their spouses or relations. As this early 19th-century copy of the original register shows, the names chosen ranged from the ordinary to the optimistically grand. Famous personages such as William Shakespeare, Francis Drake, and Inigo Jones appear alongside contemporary fictional heroes and heroines such as Pamela Andrews from Samuel Richardson's epistolary novel *Pamela* or *Virtue Rewarded*, published in 1740. As can been seen in the register, Hogarth gave his name to child no. 195, baptised 24 February 1744, while his wife Jane gave her name to child no. 265 on 5 October 1746.

20 Minutes of the General Committee
London Metropolitan Archives

These reveal the true extent of Hogarth's involvement with the Foundling Hospital, recording each meeting he attended and the numerous donations he made. These include his portrait of the Hospital's Founder *Thomas Coram* with its gold frame in 1741, *Moses brought before Pharaoh's Daughter* in 1746, and the donation of lottery tickets to the Foundling Hospital and their subsequent winning of the *March to Finchley* in 1749. Hogarth did not restrict his donations to art work but is also seen to have given £21 in 1740, a sum worth approximately £2315 today. This is no small amount and reinforces our understanding of his dedication towards the cause.

21 Letter from Ann Hogarth
London Metropolitan Archives

Mary & Ann Hogarth
*from the old Frock-shop the corner of the
Long Walk facing the Cloysters, Removed
to ĵ Kings Arms joyning to ĵ Little Britain—
gate near Long Walk. Sells ĵ best & most Fashionable Ready Made Frocks, sutes of Fustian,
Ticken & Holland, stript Dimmity & Flanel,
Wastcoats, blue & canvas Frocks, & blue coat Boys Dri-
Likewise Fustians, Tickens, Hollands, white
stript Dimitys, white & stript Flanels in ĵ piece.*
by Wholesale or Retale at Reasonable Rates.

As surviving letters such as this indicate, the interest in the Foundling Hospital was a family affair with the Hogarths. Ann Hogarth (1701-71) was William's sister who, with his other sister Jane, were in the textile business. Their shop card (*right*), designed and engraved by Hogarth, survives, and advertises that they sold 'the best & most fashionable Ready Made Frocks, sutes of Fustian, Ticken & Holland, stript Dimmity & Flannel, Wastcoats, blue & canvas Frocks' from their premises near St Bartholomew's Hospital, in the parish where they had all been born. Like Hogarth and his wife, Ann also fostered children from the Foundling Hospital. This letter outlines the expenses she has incurred for the child Mary Woodley including paying for her wet-nurse, shoes and stockings.

22 Inspector's Book
London Metropolitan Archives

Hogarth was an inspector of wet-nurses in Chiswick, where he had his country home, first being recorded in the Book of Inspectors in 1756. The hospital had decided early on to:

> … resolve to bring up the Children in General by the Breast, they should be delivered out of the Hospital to Country Nurses, as soon as proper Country Nurses can be procured, and remain with them, till they arrive at the Age of three Years.
>
> [Report of the General Committee adopted by the General Court of Governors on 1 October 1740]

The finding of wet-nurses in the countryside was a constant difficulty and the inspectors for each area were charged with the responsibility of locating women for the task.

The dispersal of the children in this way, out of central London, was an experiment on the part of the Foundling Hospital in an attempt to decrease the nearly 100% mortality rate of children kept in the city with dry-nurses. The results appear not to have been much better, and these records show that of the five children Hogarth that was responsible for in 1756 only one survived to return to the Foundling Hospital in 1761. None the less, although all of the children taken in 1757 died, two out of the three taken in 1758 survived, and were returned to the Hospital after Hogarth's death.